Identity Crisis:

The Road to Me 2.0

By Steph 2.0

Identity Crisis:

The Road to Me 2.0

Copyright 2014, Steph 2.0

All Rights Reserved

Distributed to the Kindle and Kindle-based devices by Amazon, Inc. via www.Amazon.com

Kindle is a registered trademark of Amazon, Inc.

Made in the USA.

Cover art by Isabel Sánchez-Bella

ISBN 13: 978-0692224175

Dedication

This book is dedicated to Myself.

Because I finally had the balls to be honest about who I am.

And to my precious daughter for making me laugh everyday

just because of who she is.

Love ya!

☺

Table of Contents

Prologue

Did I spell that right? It's September 2013 and suddenly I have random amount of extra time on my hands. I feel like I have a story to tell. But then I take that thought to a bird's eye view and think, hell no I don't! But you know what... maybe I do, so I'm just going to go with it. I've recently turned 40, I'm in the process of a divorce, I have a six-year old daughter (who acts like she is 16), and I was laid off three weeks ago. Anyway... it isn't pretty and even though at times I've felt completely lost I think writing is good therapy (and I am a big fan of that). I hope you see the randomness in life that comes my way, and generally see that I am a good person just trying to make my way. But with that said, how do I explain becoming inspired at random times during the day? I literately feel like I've never had the chance to experience real freedom or had extra time to express any kind of creativity. So, I'm just going to go with it. And maybe that's the point. Don't look for inspiration, let it find me.

I love Bruce Hornsby. I won tickets to his show from a radio station a long time ago, but my ex accidentally threw them away. I finally saw him at Tipitina's in New

Orleans and damn... such a great show! And now that I'm on my own, I put the Hornsby station on Pandora and ahhhh..... His songs titled Songs in H, or A, or D or whatever, oh man, just lull me into blissful relaxation like no other. It's totally true and I completely own it. Same with James Taylor. His music also has a calming effect on me. So as I write this book, I most likely am listening to Bruce or James. I'm also discovering coffee shops or little bars in the city that have great background music that work just as well for writing. Oh how I love those places! I love music and it has influenced me greatly (even as a kid). I've even thought about writing this story in song lyrics that reflect how I feel. Maybe I'll add a list of songs that move me at the end. Who knows?

And at the end of the day, what's the biggest question? I'm not sure, but what I do know is that I write exactly how I feel. (Now, there are two sides to every story, and I will say, the stories I share are only the way I saw things happen. The people in the stories may have different takes on them.) I know I'm asking to be judged, but I urge you at this point, either shut the book or commit. One or the other. Just don't leave in the middle. Neither of us will feel satisfied.

Identity Crisis – 1

I'm a twin. I'm a twin???

As the story goes, my mom was one of the "older" women having kids in 1973 (she was 36). I know, in this day in age, that's not considered old at all but back then it was. And I guess being older, you have a higher chance for giving birth to twins. She did get ultrasounds; however, the doctors thought she was going to have one big boy. OOPS! I was hiding behind my sister in the back and the doctors never saw me. My sister was born at 2:18 a.m. and I was born at 2:20 a.m. My mom went into shock. To be honest, I'm not surprised. I mean, that's quite the switch compared to what was expected. I didn't have a name for three days. I was Baby B. My brother's kindergarten class had an activity to come up with a name for me. Susan and _____. You can imagine what kindergarteners came up with. My favorite was Susan and Moosin. Thankfully, my parents came up with Stephanie. I think they were originally going to name the "big baby boy" Stephen so it made sense. Even funnier … we were born in early June, so we were born under the sign of Gemini (twins). We were double twins!

It's hard to remember when we were really little, but I think at some point we had our own special language. Obviously we were very close because as a twin you have an instant playmate. Our parents dressed us alike until we were four or five except with different hair styles. I had two side ponytails. My sister had one ponytail in the back. I don't know if we fought or not, but for a very long time we shared a bedroom.

The administrators in school were very wise not to put us in the same classrooms. That started when we were in nursery school. We were able to lobby to be in the same class when we were in the sixth grade but I'm sure that gave the teacher all kinds of headaches. Come middle school and high school, we were in a few classes together, but that was up to the computer that selected our class schedules.

We were able to make separate friends (though after school and at recess they all intertwined), but throughout our youth we did all of the same activities - swim team, dance classes, gymnastics, you name it. That was all fine and well when the activities were pretty much just about signing up for them. We generally had the same abilities when it came to activities. We are both naturally coordinated and did well, but never really excelled at anything in particular. Come the beginning of high school, we both tried out for cheerleading. That's when our differences became visible. Who knew that I liked to yell and yelling for my sister didn't come naturally. So I made the freshman squad and she didn't. Because of school zones, a small part of our eighth grade class was zoned to go to a different high school across town. We went to a new school where the majority of freshman students already knew each other. We instantly became known as "the cheerleader" and "the non-cheerleader."

Now, my sister excelled in other ways. She wasn't a cheerleader, but she went to homecoming with a football player. I was not asked and took a boy I was friends with from middle school. We each had our ups and down just as like every kid. By sophomore year, my sister made the drill team (the dance team that performed at half time at football games) and she was just as busy as I was with practice, games and camp.

The summer before our junior year we turned 16 and became legally able to work. She and I and two other friends had a crazy idea of getting our first jobs together. Circa 1988, I guess it wasn't such a farfetched idea because we all walked into Dominos and were all hired on the spot to be phone girls. That was a fun summer. The Dominos crew was quite tightknit and a lot of our summer activities revolved around that crew. I got my first boyfriend! One of my friends got one too. Generally, we all hung out together at nights and on weekends. I distinctly remember the picture of me and my sister in our Dominos shirts and hats going to work on the first day. Working at the same place sort of reinforced the "twin" thing. Probably not a good idea, but it was fun. I wouldn't recommend it now for parents of identical twins.

Because our parents were paying for two kids to go to college at the same time, they had already decided that we would both go to George Mason University. It was the cheapest school in Virginia at the time. Now, I definitely looked into going to different Virginia schools. I was very much influenced by watching college basketball and I thought John Crotty at the University of Virginia was hot stuff! I applied to James Madison, UVA, Virginia Tech, University of Richmond, and even some random schools in the Northeast. I think I was trying to see if I could get into any of them, but knew that GMU was my only option. The 40-year-old me looks at that time and says "Hey girl, if you wanted to go to another school, you should have made it happen!" But being a young 17 (and being quite shy back then) the idea of going against my parents' wishes didn't seem like a good option…

especially moneywise. I don't know. I think back then I just wasn't sure of who I was or what I was capable of.

And so it goes, we both got accepted to GMU and for the first year, to save money, we lived at home and commuted to school - SHARING THE SAME CAR! This was such a bad idea. I mean, sure it saved money, but it definitely exacerbated the "twin" thing in the way of always having to be together in some way. I met my first college boyfriend at orientation, so I ended up spending a lot of time with him in the freshmen dorms. A fair number of high school folks were in freshmen dorms and my sister and I would hang out with them.

Sometime that fall my sister and I both tried out for the GMU dance team. Of course we tried out together, so our dance timing was spot on and we both made the squad. The team danced during halftime at the basketball games and in the summer, the team went to dance camp. The team would practice three nights a week starting in the fall. It was a fairly big time commitment. We both stayed on the team for the next three years. In fact, during our sophomore year an article written about us in a university newspaper that reported on the happenings at all DC area colleges. The newspaper thought it was cute that we were on the team together, and titled the article "GMU Twins Dancing Double Time." YIKES! It talked about how we were both on the dance team, lived in the dorms together, had the same major and were in the same sorority. Kind of scary looking back at that article... I mean, good god, we definitely needed separate identities!

As noted above, in the fall of our sophomore year we both went through Sorority Rush. We were accepted into three different sororities, but one of the top ones was Chi Omega - the one with all of the twins. I think it had four sets of twins as sisters. It was definitely known as the "twin" sorority on campus. My freshmen boyfriend was in a fraternity, so both my sister and I already had been a part of Greek life. Going through Rush just sort of made it official.

Starting our sophomore year, we moved on campus and never moved back home ... not even for the summers. (That says a lot - meaning we would be willing to sublet someone's place for the summer rather than live for free at home.) That first year, we lived in Dominion Hall. We tried to live together, but when the school picked roommates, we were not put together. I know we were pissed about that, and tried to switch, but the RA wouldn't let us. I had a nightmare of a roommate and side roommate (two rooms attached with a bathroom, four people in total), and tried not to spend too much time there. Junior year we were allowed to move into the on-campus apartments, where six people could live together. Of course, my sister was one of them. And guess what? We shared a room! Come on... just nuts! It was our choice, but I think you can start to see the pattern... we lived in the apartments our senior year, again sharing a room.

By junior year, students had to declare a major and guess what... we BOTH chose accounting. Go figure! We were both good at math and logic. It didn't bother me that we were taking the same path in life. I mean, it was how it always was. We had some of the same professors. Towards the end of college, we started interviewing for the same jobs. We would interview right after another. The recruiters would say "We just met you!" Dumb, just dumb. Parents of twins... take note of this. Make sure your twins start with separate identities early in life before it's engrained into who each one is.

Somehow it was perceived that I was offered the better job: in public accounting. My sister received an offer from a corporation. Back in the mid-1990s, the first job an accounting major was expected to have was one in public accounting. And so it was... I got a job working at the CPA firm and she didn't.

We both took an extra half year to graduate to finish last classes and worked at part-time jobs. And guess what? We lived in a group apartment off campus. We stayed in that house for two years. Many of our friends were a year younger than us, so when they graduated, we moved to a different house. There were four of us and we hung out all the time. Sometime that fall I broke up with my two-year college boyfriend. I ended up being single for a whole nine months, changed jobs and then met my now ex-husband. I met him in spring 1998, and by the end of that summer I moved into DC.

After looking back and being much wiser now, I can see how much emotional damage moving into DC may have done to my sister. If it's engrained in you to be with another person for so much in life (starting at birth) the decision to be with the person who I thought was the man of my dreams could have been pretty devastating for her. But that's her journey to speak about... not mine.

Identity Crisis – 2

Married? I'm married!!

I met my ex-husband (now to be referred as "the Ex") in March 1998 at my favorite bar in the world: Madams Organ in DC. It's actually a pretty funny story. My old roommate had met a guy at a 70's themed bar in DC, Polyesters, the previous weekend. That guy had a thing for red-headed girls, and asked to see her the next weekend. I distinctly remember being in sweats at 9 p.m. and my roommate asked my sister and I to go with her to meet the guy, as he was bringing a group of friends. We didn't get there until midnight, walked all around the bar and he finally tracked her down. My sister and I met that dude and his friends that consisted of the Ex and two other friends. The group all hung out that night, and during that time, I was used to guys wanting to dance with my sister, not me. We both talked to the Ex and he told us that he was three months out of an engagement (red flag... Big Red Flag) and was moving into the city. At some point during the night, my sister and I went to the bathroom and talked. We both thought the Ex was cute and said no one could have him and shook hands on it. It was the first time that we thought the same guy was cute. We left the bathroom and then the Ex asked to me to dance. So we danced for a while, and then he asked for my number but I said no. See, in my short single life, I was tired of giving out my number and not getting a call. I got his number instead. I think for a while my sister was mad about that, but now, at age 40, she should thank her lucky stars it was me who got together with him, not her.

At the time I didn't have a cell phone and worked in a cube at a hotel corporation. I didn't want to make "the call" and have everyone at work hear me, so I drove home at lunch all the way from Bethesda to Fairfax to make the call. I picked lunchtime assuming that he would be at lunch and I could just leave a message. Oops, he answered! I said "Ugh, ugh, hi, I'm the girl you met on Saturday night," and we talked briefly about going to dinner. I said "Yes." Now, I knew he had enormous amount of baggage that I didn't want to deal with, but I thought … it's just dinner. As you would expect the dinner was very fun and by the third date I told him I loved him. Now I know that there is no way in hell you can love a person after Date #3. What I was feeling was that being with him just made me feel good. That's what I was expressing. However, to a guy just out of an engagement (that he didn't want to end), I'm sure it sounded like magic, and away we went. Suddenly we were together all the time, and by the end of the summer, I had moved to DC. I was always driving to the city to see him so moving into DC was easier (he didn't have a car). I became immersed in his guy friends and their girlfriends. I remember feeling disappointed that we were not engaged that December. Crazy thoughts! We moved in together in 2000, he asked me to marry him in March 2001, and we planned the wedding for May 2002.

He started working at a law firm after working for the government, and I was doing SEC financial reporting at a hotel company in Georgetown. We were one of the first couples in our group of friends to get married, and constantly went to see live music, go out with friends, and do some traveling. We became the center of our group of friends, and whenever we would go out and meet more people, the group got bigger. Everyone we knew would ask "How do you know that person?" Always the answer seemed to be - the Ex or Steph. We even planned our wedding to be a big party in Key West. Friends from the West Coast and East Coast converged in Key West between Tuesday and Friday of our wedding week. By the time of our wedding on Saturday, many new friendships were formed. Lots of intercostal hooking up happened as well. (Oh, the stories!!)

(I did have an incident with the Ex's sister on the Wednesday of our wedding week. Somehow she thought it was ok to randomly tell me that if we ever had kids, they would be flat chested. I just thought that was so inappropriate. I was being judged on the size of my boobs? Huh?? I'm a petite girl!! I went to our hotel room and I got really upset. The Ex told me it wasn't a big deal and that his sister was just kidding. I expected him to have my back. I remember telling my sister: If this is how it's going to be, I don't know if I could do this. But with three days to go to the wedding and our lives being so intertwined it was just forgotten.)

Anyway, our wedding was so much fun, but not without mishaps. I had a weird tickle in my stomach the whole day, worrying something would happen. After the ceremony and pictures, our photographer fell off the pier with three cameras in tow. No joke. Luckily one of our guests was a photographer, and all went well in the end. I was able to relax after that mishap and finally get my party on! Needless to say, people were on the dance floor before the food was served. At some point the bar ran out of liquor. You can imagine that type of wedding - classy but casual and lots of dancing. Everyone said they had a great time! Which is what we wanted. I remember how the

Ex looked at me when he said his vows with a look of love in his eyes. I remember that to this day. However, over time, that love slowly faded away and there was nothing I could do about it.

See, I was never the little girl that dreamed about my wedding day, the man of my dreams, or any of it. I was going with what I thought was a good stable relationship, and followed what society says to do. Go to college, graduate, get a job, meet a boy, get engaged, and get married. I really thought I had it all, and nothing was ever going to change. I had my job, our condo, a marriage, a cute dog, and a car. What else could there be? That's the perfect life, as society says. I was married!

Identity Crisis - 3

Living in the burbs? Yep, living in the burbs.

We got married in May 2002, and started looking at houses that summer. I wasn't ready to move, but the Ex liked real estate and started seeing good deals. We looked at two houses in the Friendship Heights neighborhood of DC. We actually saw the second house on September 11, 2002, so there was barely anyone at the open house. We won the contract, and by November 2002, we moved into a cute little brick house in upper northwest DC. Mind you... it's not the suburbs by any means, but it was two blocks from the Maryland line, so kind of far from the action. I cried for two weeks before we moved. Change is hard for me. It just is.

The house needed a lot of work and the Ex could see the vision, but it just gave me anxiety. Quickly our life became about renovations. We renovated the kitchen (while living there - that was crazy), opened up the back sunroom with French doors, added a deck, put a hot tub in the back yard, and completely renovated the basement. The Ex really enjoyed it as he is super handy, but for me, inside I felt something dying. I remember thinking... ok, so this is it? We spent endless amounts of time researching renovations and going to hardware stores. And because we also held onto the condo, he was always dealing with the tenant or doing an open house. The Ex was the manager of the property and that took up some time. I just became more excited to travel.

Luckily, we were able to take two different two-week trips in 2004 and 2005. The first one was Italy and Greece, and the second, Portugal and Spain. I think that tickled an urge in me for experiences rather than material items. We had a great time, and the second trip was the first time I let myself wing it and not plan everything. It was the first time I found that letting go of expectations can sometimes make for better times.

I didn't realize it back then, but all I know is that for me, the house made me feel empty. We always hosted parties. I loved having people over to celebrate something. It was work to have the parties, but why not show off all the work we did on the house, right? Once the house was done, what was next... The Ex was still interested in real estate, so we bought a property in Atlantic City with another couple. For most of late 2005 and early 2006, we would drive to Atlantic City every weekend to do renovations. Sometime we would bring up friends, which was fun. But it became the same thing... endlessly going to the hardware store, and driving up and back. Yes, we had some good times, but for me, there was just something missing, and I didn't know what it was or how to express it.

Identity Crisis - 4

Can I be a mom??? Yes I can.

Like never dreaming of a wedding, I never had a gut feeling that I had to get pregnant and to have a baby. I'm not sure why. I just didn't. Maybe I was scared, or maybe it was the changes related to having a kid. But it was the next logical thing you do in married life, so I had the bright idea of teaming up with two other girlfriends to all try to get pregnant at the same time. Deep down I knew I would not be able to talk to the Ex about the experiences of a woman trying to get pregnant, so I thought having a good sounding board with a couple of women would be a good idea. That ended up being a very bad idea.

There are many women out there who suffer from infertility. Many, as I did, suffer in silence. As the story goes, sometime in 2005, I went off the pill. I had been on the pill since I was 18, and I was on it for 13 years or so. I had heard that once you get off the pill it could be very easy to get pregnant. Problem was that when I went off the Pill, I never got my period. Not once. I never got out of the starting gate. I went to specialists, took all kinds of drugs to get my body to do its thing. I had every bad side effect and zero results. It was awful. I was a raging bitch and the Ex had zero understanding of what the drugs were doing to me. I think that is when our marriage started to come apart at the seams. Or at least when the clear communication between us began to fade.

I knew deep down there was something medically wrong with me, but not one doctor could figure it out. My entire being became about being able to get pregnant. It was all I could think about, and I constantly felt like a failure. I couldn't make regular decisions because I thought that some point in the future I might be pregnant. Can I take a trip? Can I get a new job? All I saw were pregnant women everywhere I went, and somehow I overheard even the faintest of conversations about pregnancy. I felt paralyzed. I started seeing a therapist.

After nine months of working with specialists and taking drugs with no results, we considered IVF. The doctors explained how much estrogen it would take, and I decided then and there, that there was no way I could put my body through that. Clearly my body had a different idea of things. So I gave the reigns to the Ex to research adoption while I just relaxed and focused on my new job.

That part was good - finally he was able to do something. He researched domestic and international adoptions. We ended up deciding on international because I didn't like the idea of having to sell myself and prove I'd be a good mom. Plus I wanted to be the mom. I didn't want to feel like there was a second mom. So we started with the Russian program. We did background checks, home study... the works. It took about six months of tracking down and filling out the paperwork. By January 2007 we were ready. After two weeks we switched from the Russian program to the Guatemalan one as we were afraid of fetal alcohol syndrome. See, at first I was just hell bent on having my kid look like me no matter what, but really at the end of the day, I just wanted to have a healthy kid. That's it. The paperwork was submitted so we sat back... and waited.

Coincidentally, once I let go of trying to get pregnant, I was much happier and relaxed. I ended up going to a new primary doctor. She looked at my thyroid numbers and said "Hmmm ... the number looks a bit high; maybe we should put you on medication?" At that point I still wasn't having a period. I had learned to accept that was my body was going to do what it was going to do—even though underneath it still felt like something was wrong with me as a woman. Low and behold, after three months of being on the medicine I got my period! I was so shocked and elated. I felt like a woman again. Turns out my thyroid levels were in fact within the normal range, but not in the normal range for me.

In April 2007, the Ex and I went to a baseball game and I suddenly felt like I had a urinary tract infection. I didn't want to wait until Monday to go to the doctor so we stopped at GW hospital. The doctor came to in and asked "Do you know if you are pregnant?? Your hormone levels suggest you are". I said... what? I'm so confused, we are adopting! So on Monday I went to the doctor to get my hormones checked. On Wednesday I went to get an ultrasound and found out that it was a blighted ovum (my body thought it was pregnant and was getting ready for a baby but there was nothing inside). By Friday I was at Sibley Hospital having a D&C done. (Noticeably the Ex wasn't there. A meeting in Boston was more important.) It was crazy! People said they were sorry for my miscarriage and I said "No way. This was great." I finally felt like a real woman!

Funny enough, my sister had the same thyroid issue as I did. However, she had her thyroid fixed with medication before she tried to get pregnant and gave birth to a healthy baby girl in 2011.

In August 2007, we heard from the adoption agency that we were matched with a two-week old baby girl in Guatemala. We saw pictures and a short video. So we took the leap of faith... that baby girl was going to be our daughter. I remember the day the Ex and I met on the street and made the decision. I am a planner at heart, and taking that leap was really hard. Now I know it was the best thing I could have ever done. But I certainly didn't trust myself at that point, and I felt something in the pit in my stomach. A big change was a-coming.

We would get pictures each week as she grew. We knew the adoption program in Guatemala could be shut down at the end of 2007, so didn't do anything to get ready for the baby. From August to December we didn't let ourselves get attached at all. Come January, we found out that the program was, in fact, shutdown but we were grandfathered into the program so the adoption was set. We got her room ready quickly, flew to Guatemala in February to meet her, and then four weeks later, flew back to Guatemala to bring her home. It was like I became an instant mom. I remember I had been lifting five-pound weights at the gym. My girl was 16 pounds when we brought her home! I was not ready for that. I remember thinking: I'm supposed to take care of her?

(I'm sure every new parent thinks that whether giving birth or adopting.) I had no confidence whatsoever. I never felt comfortable interacting with kids before, and now here was the real deal.

We got home and I took three months off of work to bond with my daughter. Funny enough, the experience was completely different than a newborn. My daughter has always been a great sleeper and at eight months she was taking three naps a day and sleeping a full night. I can honestly say at times I was bored. I was surprised at that. She just slept so much that I was just left to think about things, what I should be doing…

I remember taking her on walks and feeling like I was advertising my infertility. My daughter does not look like me, and I had numerous strangers ask if she was my child. I think having so much extra time to think and the feeling of constantly be judged took its toll. By the end of the three months at home, I literally had panic attacks whenever I took a walk with her to Starbucks or CVS. It happened every day. I couldn't talk to the Ex about it as all he would say is "Don't you want to be with your daughter?" Of course I did, but I had no idea what I was doing, felt ashamed for not knowing, and was constantly being asked if she was my kid. My general anxiety went into overtime and took over my body. Luckily, my sister had gone through something similar and suggested I go see a specialist. I made the phone call, and I'm glad I did. I started taking the necessary drugs and it was very helpful. My daughter went into daycare in September 2008, and away we went into being a two working parent household with a young daughter and a dog.

Identity Crisis - 5

Married?? Nope, not married.

Slowly, very slowly, the trials of parenting a very young daughter and working full-time made me exhausted. I think I was trying to prove to the world that I was a great mom and I could do it all - drop off, pick up, cooking, bedtime, and work with tight deadlines. I was so tired all the time. The Ex had to travel for work, had to work late at times, and took up road biking to work off stress. I completely supported that. I realized now that I completely enabled him to become disconnected with me. Like every guy, he wanted sex. I was so tired that sex never even entered my mind. It really didn't. I wasn't attracted to him or anyone else for that matter. I was focused on being a mom. And maybe because my daughter was adopted, I felt like I REALLY needed to prove that I was a great mom. So when the Ex started going out with his friends on the weekends until 2 or 3 a.m., I just didn't care. It didn't bother me at all. It didn't bother me that he would then get up for a long bike ride in the early morning, come home, and fall asleep on the couch.

By the time that our daughter turned two I remember thinking... OK, I'm settled into the mom role, now I want my life back. Meaning that I realized I still wanted experiences for myself. I couldn't just be mom, wife, and worker. I wanted a piece of my life just for me. How to get that back I didn't know. And unfortunately, I wasn't able to clearly communicate with the Ex. There was always something else more important, and when I did have the chance to talk to him, I just shut down and didn't say anything. I felt judged because in his eyes, any emotion was wrong. I blame that on him being a lawyer. I think that is how a lawyer is trained in law school, to always, always, always take the opposite opinion, no matter what.

Because the Ex was so busy, it would always just be me and my daughter hanging around the neighborhood. I felt like an asshole putting on a fake face to show that all was just fine. It wasn't. I felt like I was parenting all by myself with zero support from the Ex and no one to talk to about it. I would sit on the couch and watch the Ex go out and I'd say "I want to go out too!" He told me I needed new friends. Now, I can't say what happened when he went out with his friends, but I'm sure he got a lot of attention from women and probably once he got that, it became a bit addictive. I completely get that. Everyone wants a human connection, and I wasn't giving him one. I wasn't giving him one because I didn't feel an emotional connection with him. Classic downfall of a marriage with a young kid. I'm not sure if he wanted me to get in his face and say "Don't go out!" but for some reason, I felt so shut down that I couldn't say anything. I didn't want another night of him looking at me with the expectation of sex and I had no desire whatsoever. It is what it is now.

The simple explanation is that for me communication = sex, for him sex = communication. Woman vs. man. Classic downfall. What I do know now is that if you stick it out and communicate, you might be able to get out of the rut because young kids get older and more independent and the stress you feel after no sleep and working full time will ease as time goes on. It just didn't work like that for us.

Come December 2009, our precious dog, Libby, became sick. We had adopted her in 2000 as a five-year-old beagle from Puerto Rico. She had a huge tumor in her stomach and had to have emergency surgery. I remember us taking her to the animal hospital at 2 a.m. with our daughter in tow and Libby panting on my lap. We made it just in time. She made it through surgery and recovered nicely. She had the spring back in her step and that was great to see. In late December, the Ex had a work trip and the first of several blizzards hit DC. I was home by myself with a two-and-a-half year old and a dog. Literally, I had to shovel the front and back every hour on the hour to keep it clear. I had to have my daughter get dressed, entertained and outside with me shoveling. By 5 p.m. I was in tears. I didn't know who to ask for help. It was so hard. Luckily the next morning our nice neighbors cleared off the car... Merry Christmas! I was so thankful for that.

In January 2010, Libby took a turn for the worse and the tumor came back. We took her to her favorite places in and out of town and slowly watched her deteriorate. I wanted to put her to sleep a week before the Ex was ready. Libby would just sleep and not eat and the Ex would try to spoon-feed her. So sad to watch. All I knew is I wanted to be there when she died, I didn't want to come home to a dead dog. Finally the Ex agreed. We took her to a vet in Leesburg and it happened. Honestly, finally seeing her body at peace made me feel better. I hated seeing her suffer. She was cremated with her bed and her ashes sit on the Ex's mantle.

Walking back into the house with no dog that was constantly there for 10 years was incredibility hard to do. It was the first time I saw the Ex cry. But at that point, communication between the Ex and I was very, very little. So he grieved in his way, I grieved in mine. Two blizzards came and every day the Ex shoveled every sidewalk in the neighborhood. Clearly that was his way of dealing with it. I, in turn, wrote a tribute to Libby and posted it on the dog adoption's website. Oddly enough, back in 2001, the Ex had written a post for that same website on how great it was to have Libby and how much joy she brought us. To this day my daughter talks about how much she misses Libby.

Fast forward to fall of 2010 when we adopted a new beagle we named Surrey, I started thinking that I wanted a connection with the Ex again. I started planning date nights for us ... the whole works. And over time, I realized that I only wanted to go out when there was someone else there. I didn't enjoy my alone time with him, and I believe he felt the same thing. He was so tired from the week and doing his thing and I was so eager to let off steam that we didn't connect at all. It was the beginning of the end taking hold. But when you are married for so long, what do you do? You do what many couples do... pretend.

Since I love experiences I always planned an annual girls' trip. It was the only time I had a chance to travel. And truth be told, as I started to pretend to be happy in my marriage, I started drinking more. I had no one to talk to about my failed marriage and I felt ashamed that I was resigned to a life of being unhappy and faking it. Anyway, spring 2011, the girls planned the annual girls trip to Puerto Rico. Six girls went, and it was nice to be away with zero responsibility. All the other girls were calling their husbands to check in on how the kids and everything at home was doing. I called the Ex and all I got was "Why are you calling me so much?"

I was calling to check in as the Ex's hand was severely wounded after being bitten by a dog the afternoon I left for vacation, my daughter witnessed the whole bloody thing, and she spent hours at a neighbor's house because he was at urgent care. Call me crazy for checking in on my family.

That did it. The second night I drank too much at dinner, went to the lobby bar with the girls, and some guy started flirting with me, telling me I was hot, pretty, and funny. I literally was like "Tell me again!" It almost was like a drug… it felt so damn good! I left the hotel with him and hooked up (not all the way, but in a way that I wanted). It literally could have been any guy. He wasn't super good looking or anything, he just said the right things. Anyway, I felt very guilty about it. I had been in numerous situations like that before, but when you are in a good relationship, you don't do anything. It's harmless flirting. Clearly I had crossed a line. (Side bar: The flight home was instantly called the Best Flight Ever - a great story, but best for another time.)

So when I got home I didn't think it would be helpful to come clean. I tried to figure it out thinking it was a onetime thing. Problem was the Ex found out via my friend's phone and probably felt so ashamed that he couldn't say anything to me. I'm not sure. All I know is he sat on the information for three months and then told me he knew via text while I was at work and he was out of town. Really, really awful. That hardest part was going to pick up my daughter, put a fake smile on my face when all I wanted to do was cry my eyes out. I begged for us to go to counseling. We went two times and it was over. The sessions were all about me - how he wasn't sure he wanted to be with a person like me and for the past 10 years he's been trying to fix me. While I'm certainly not perfect, a work in progress I suppose, I don't need "fixing". But I was so afraid of pulling the plug on my "happy married life" that I just went along. The reason why the Puerto Rico event even happened in the first place was never discussed and it became the big elephant in the room. It was really hard to fake a front, feel like crap on the inside, and watch the Ex do his thing.

Now I will refrain from the ugliness that ensued on both sides. I fully own all the stuff I did and with this book I'm certainly not trying to paint the Ex as a bad man. We just were not right for each other and couldn't communicate. But I will say, it was not easy. Not easy at all!

In December 2011, the Ex went to California for the winter holidays with my daughter, and I stayed home. One night that week I went to dinner with two girlfriends and, no joke, the diamond on my engagement ring broke off. In January 2012, he moved to the basement to sleep at night and continued to do whatever he wanted. Somehow my daughter never knew he was sleeping in the basement. My parents saw me and the stress I was under and said "You need to do something about this as it is going to kill you." They didn't know any details, but clearly the stress was easy to see.

In March 2012 we went to my daughter's preschool to celebrate her "gotcha day" (the day she was adopted and we became a family), and it felt so fake. That night I manned up and finally confronted the Ex on how unhappy we both were. He couldn't give me what I wanted, and I couldn't give him what he wanted. I said we needed to have an open marriage or get divorced. I started going out like he did. I think that caught him off guard. I went to Jazz Fest in New Orleans for the annual girls' trip in April 2012 for four nights, partied my ass off, came back to DC and stayed at a hotel for three additional nights. I started to enjoy who I was without him. I liked the freedom to be me. The night I had to go back to the house I was in tears. The next day at work I signed a lease for a very expensive apartment that I had never seen. I don't do that. Never. But the stress pushed me to do it - my inner voice. I moved out of our little brick house in June 2012.

So at this point, I was technically married, but not married. I never ever thought my relationship would end up like that. However, looking back you can see all the red flags, all the pretending. That does not make a good relationship at all. I was so young when I met him and I didn't have a clue who I was at all. I think things happen for a reason. There is a reason I met the Ex and was on that journey. But it was time to end that journey and start doing what I wanted to do in life.

Telling my daughter and the actual process of moving out was very, very stressful. I remember the day we were going to tell our daughter. I felt sick all day. I went home from work at noon and took a nap. I had a very vivid dream. The "family" and extended family were all in the house with a storm brewing. It was a black and white film. Dark clouds came in, the wind was howling, and everyone huddled together. And the movie cut to a different movie - one of 1940s fighter planes, ahead of the storm. The planes dropped a bomb on the house. And the dream cut to black. I woke up in tears and sweat. Clearly I was stressed about telling her.

I had to push back my move-out date by a couple of days because of the Ex's work travel. It happened to coincide with the same week my daughter graduated from pre-school. Really bad timing. Due to me moving out I hadn't seen her in a couple of days and I showed up at the recital at her preschool. The show started, she came out with her class, saw me and just froze. In the middle of the performance she just started to cry pointing at me. She ran off stage to me and I hugged her. The Ex said she was just hungry.

We had planned a graduation dinner at one of my favorite restaurant/bar, Chadwick's, with three other kids and their parents. It was a great dinner, the kids had a great time, and suddenly a nasty storm blew in. The Ex got a call from a neighbor saying a tree had fallen down and the power was out at his house. He ran back to the house and I stayed with the group. He really didn't have power, but I was not in a place to have my daughter at my new apartment yet. (I was still in boxes and according to therapists, it was important that she NOT see me unsettled.) Thankfully one of the other couples knew what was going on and offered to take our daughter for a sleepover. I am indebted to this couple - they saved the day! After that, I went over to the old house to find that a huge tree had fallen directly on the car and directly in front of the front door. What are the odds of that? We had lived there for 10 years and not once had that ever happened before.

What did give me solace after I moved out was that I randomly I started seeing the numbers 777. It happened three times. First when I was getting yogurt with my daughter (the kind you serve yourself and get to put whatever you want on top) and the bill was $7.77. The cashier told me I should play the lottery. The second was when I went on a random date with a dude and we got sushi and our bill was $77.77. The third was when I got the overage utility cost from the short period I was in my apartment: June 21 – June 30. The bill was $7.77. I kept thinking, what in the world? Turns out, after researching it online, seems like it's the energy around me is saying I'm doing the right thing. I absolutely think things happen for a reason. I don't see 777 a lot still, but when I do, it gives me a sense of calm.

Mind you, I did spend the entire July 4th holiday in bed with a migraine headache. I hadn't had a migraine since I was studying for the CPA exam! Essentially, it was my body letting go all of all the stress I'd been holding on to. I can't say I'm surprised. Moving out was the hardest thing I've ever done in my life. I knew it would directly hurt our daughter, but I didn't have a choice. The Ex wasn't changing and I was suffocating.

The divorce will be final on February 13, 2014, at 9:30 a.m. What are the odds the official end is the day before Valentine's Day?

Identity Crisis - 6

I'm a CPA. I'm a CPA???

As I grew up, I always appreciated math more than writing. I think I was drawn to it because math has concrete answers. I was a very shy kid, and being judged in a way for something subjective, like writing, was pretty hard for me. I'm ok with it now as I'm writing this book. But taking a look back, somehow numbers made sense to me, and I really liked that there were set answers to problems.

I remember my accounting class in high school. It was a subject that I did well in and didn't have to push myself. Granted, some accounting classes were hard in college, but it was nice to find something that made sense and wasn't too hard. My dad had it imprinted on my sister and I that we needed a market place skill, and accounting fit the bill.

I got my first job out of college and studied for the CPA exam. I was told, back in the day, the exam was harder than the Bar exam. Probably right. Back in the late 1990s, you had to take all four parts all at one time, and I think there were only four times to take the test in a year. Really hard stuff. It was a two-day test. I remember studying all the time, trying to memorize. In the end, personally, I think it came down to luck, whatever part you studied the last time. Now, plenty of people mastered the exam the first or second round. There were a fair amount of people that it took several times. It took me maybe four times to pass. What I do remember is the ethics test sent in the mail. I think I took that damn thing 10 times! You had to get a 90% to pass it and each time I got 88%. I would study what I got wrong, submit it again, and I still couldn't pass the test. Thankfully, I finally received a letter in the mail that said there were actually a couple of answers that had two correct answers, so I finally passed. The problem was the actual test, not my intellectual abilities.

Well, once a CPA, a CPA you are. I really did like numbers and I was good at it. But I hated public accounting. Being crazy busy for four months of the year and then no work to do felt odd. Granted, I had some good times in public accounting, and I have some good stories. I ended up hooking up with a coworker but couldn't handle the stress that came with that. Within two months after that, I left that job to work for a hotel company. Funny, I thought that hook up was something special. Nope. I definitely learned from that one.

I enjoyed my new job, and really enjoyed actually being able to pull a whole financial statement together rather than piecemeal. I met some interesting folks, but after I met the Ex, I really wanted to work in DC and found another hotel company that was headquartered in Georgetown. I was there from December 1998 through 2005. I really enjoyed that company, the entrepreneurial style it had, and the fun. If I could work for that CFO again, I would in a heartbeat. He was awesome. The kind of guy that didn't leave if I had to work late. He stuck around to make sure the work was done too. The roll-up-your-sleeves kind of person. The happy hours were great, the top-notch grilled cheese Fridays, and the earnings call with everyone in one room listening. I really enjoyed it. I laughed my ass off, but worked hard. And everyone else did the same.

The company owned and operated hotels around the country, and after a few years, it was decided that the two divisions would split. So, I had to pick which to go with, and decided to stay with the part of the company that owned the hotels. In the summer of 2001, the employees found out that the company was going to merge with a company in Dallas and most of the jobs were going to move to Dallas, Texas.

Obviously, that was not what I signed up for. Then September 11, 2001 happened.

I remember that day so vividly. I went to work, heard about the first tower, got coffee, heard about the second tower, called the Ex, looked out the window, and saw smoke from the Pentagon. I completely freaked out. It felt like the world had turned upside down. I said "Screw this, I'm leaving!" So I got in my car to go home. DC was in utter gridlock. I only made it to around George Washington Circle on K Street. I really thought about abandoning my car. I couldn't get in touch with anyone because of the bad cell phone service. I remember listening to the radio and hearing about the fourth plane. I heard fighter jets above. But I swear to god I thought, this is it. It's the fourth plane and no one knows where I am. Very, very scary. But it wasn't, I survived and witnessed some really great stuff on my drive home. I saw people walking, walking, and walking. I saw restaurant employees walking outside with Dixie cups full of water for the walkers. I saw ordinary people become traffic cops. Really amazing. I breathed a sigh of relief when I got home after inching along for 2 hours. Our condo was right near the Israeli embassy so that freaked me out and I had a distinct urge to move out of DC. It was really weird to go to work and see the military on K Street with machine guns. It did make things feel safe, but still an odd sight to see.

That said, due to September 11, the companies pulled out of the merger deal and I kept my job. However, the thought of possibly losing my job to a potential merger scarred me. I always thought that a job in accounting was secure, but you know what, it's not. Nothing is.

I enjoyed my job until the Enron debacle happened. Suddenly, everything was hyper-scrutinized, everyone on the board of directors had to have value-added comments in the financial statements, the deadlines were severely crunched and in the end, and I ended up feeling like a word processer. I mean, there are only so many ways to say the same thing, but everyone was running scared. By 2005 I had enough and decided to look for something else. The type of work wasn't going to change, so I had to make the change.

I ended up working for another publicly traded company, which was a horrible working environment, but I have friends from that job to this day. I lasted barely two years there and guess what, the company was sold. I was a CPA, with what I felt like a secure market place skill, but was still getting the rug pulled out from under me. I decided at that point, I want to work for a company that couldn't be sold.

In July 2006 I started working at a non-profit with a great mission statement. I really enjoyed my job, supporting a specific product area. The group I was in reminded of me when I worked with the hotel company back in early 2000. A work hard, play hard kind of place. Lots of laughing about absurd things. I enjoyed going to work. I remember discussing the Obama 2008 election at length. It truly was a pleasure to go to work every day. My boss was cool, her boss was cool, the girl who worked for me was great, and my cube neighbor was awesome. It was just a fun place to be!

My boss and others were very supportive when we adopted our daughter. I have pictures of her when she was very young and at my computer. I remember her crawling on the floor there. That is the only job I've had since we adopted her. As she has grown up, she grew to love where I worked. She loved the museum, the store, and the cafeteria. But, alas, all good things must come to an end.

As my marriage began to unravel, work became a source of stability for me. My outside life was going nuts, but at least that was a place where I knew what

I was doing. Unfortunately, my job was eventually absorbed into a different area of the company and my skill level was not appreciated there. I still worked for the same people but the different higher ups didn't understand what I did on a day-to-day basis, and in late August 2013 I was laid off. A gigantic bummer. I really enjoyed the people I supported, and the group I worked for never had a problem with me, just the higher ups. Yes, I talked a bit much, I laughed at really dumb things, and my laugh was loud, but getting in trouble for that is just dumb in my book. But it's over.

So at the end of the day, I'm a CPA? I guess I am. I was trained to be a CPA, but at this juncture in my life, I'm wondering if that is what I should be. I mean, I am good with numbers, but I just don't have a personality of a CPA. I'm not sorry about that, it's just who I am. Now I'm trying to figure out how to make that work in the working world of 2014. Maybe I'll get a job supporting small businesses in DC. Who knows? But at least for now, I think I might be done with the corporate world.

However, I am my father's daughter, and I sure as hell am afraid of doing what he did (he started his own insurance business that went south when my sister and I were in middle school). But at least for now I'm going to trust my gut, and, for once in my life, see what happens. Eek! Not easy, but I'm going with it. Should I be afraid? Should I do what I want to do? Can you hear the anxiety? It's all wrapped up in me. Point is, that is when I started the Road to Me 2.0. I am now starting to listen to my gut despite what conventional wisdom says or what society says. I'm doing things that make sense to ME now. And, boy, is that an odd feeling. I'm trying to stay the course. I get gun shy wondering if I'm doing the right thing.

Identity Crisis - 7

I'm a mom? Yes, I am a MOM!

It's been a slow process, but as I became more confident in my skills as a parent, it seems the bond with my daughter has vastly improved and has become very strong. It's funny, I never knew my face had so many expressions. As it turns out my daughter has completely picked up on them. Once she was about five years old, I got less and less questions about whether she was my daughter. People would just say "Yep, that's your daughter! She looks like you!" and I can see what they mean. She talks to me about everything she feels, and I'm happy to say that I am the one that knows her the best. I know what makes her tick.

She's a true perfectionist, and if something doesn't come easily to her she quickly gets frustrated and she doesn't try. When her confidence is up she figures things out very quickly. She didn't walk until she was 18 months old, but the day she stood up was the day she walked, and she looked like she was walking for months. Same for potty training. Same for learning in school. What I've learned is that one-on-one tutoring works wonders for her. However, if the tutor is me, forget it. By being a perfectionist, she wants to show me that she already knows how to do something. She doesn't want me to see that she tries and messes up. I tell her no one is perfect and never will be. I just have to remember - she is hard wired as such and if I push, it's a waste of time. When she's ready, she's ready. My pushing only frustrates both of us.

I'm happy to show off our bond as mom and daughter even though it's not via blood. I feel very protective of her, and if I get a sniff of anyone being mean to her or an adult looking at her weird, or anything, I feel this tiger mom feeling rise up in me. I know I'm raising her to be a fighter, to be vocal. Now granted, she is so much more artistic than I was as a kid. And I am being cognizant of that. However, seeing how I'm showing her how not to be shy, to be friendly, and open, I can't help feeling that somehow I'm seeing how I may have been when I was a kid.

Everyone says she seems mature beyond her years, she's beautiful, she acts older, she's smart, and very, very funny. (I've been keeping a list of her quotes and they are outstandingly funny!) I feel this overwhelming pride in her. I know that her huge personality will be tapped into whatever job she chooses when she gets older. Currently, she seems to have a fondness for how music gets on the radio, how movies are made, and what TV shows she wants to be on someday. So we will see. Maybe she'll be discovered one of these days. There's got to be a talent in all her talking! And, thank goodness, she does talk to me. She told me "You know Mom, I was pretending when I said I was happy you moved out." Not surprised. ☹

We've always talked openly with her about her adoption, and now at six-and-a-half she is starting to figure out her identity. She asks me why she doesn't speak Spanish, what color of skin my prom dates were, and says she wants to dye her hair like mine. I tell her I want her hair, however, just like the Lady Gaga song, we are all just "Born this Way." No one is perfect, no one ever will be. I co-host a monthly support group for general infertility and brought my daughter to one meeting. I know we made an impact on the folks at the meeting - really showing them what a mom and daughter look like, no matter how it happens. My daughter was a bit shy, but I was proud to show her that I was helping people. In the future, I'd like to find a volunteering opportunity that we both can do together occasionally. I plan to take her to Guatemala when she's around 10 to see and experience her heritage first hand.

I want to raise her to be conscious of others around her and to know that the world doesn't revolve around just her. I refuse to let her grow up feeling entitled to have the easy road because of who she is. She will have to learn from her mistakes, put her chin up, move forward, and enjoy life. Life sure can test you at times, but in the end, it's all about perspective and realizing you can brush off the dust and be a better person because you have the strength inside to do so. My girl is a fighter through and through. Just like her mom. ☺

Moving Forward

As I move forward with my life, there are only a couple things I'm sure about: 1) I hope to help and inspire people in one way or the other and 2) I want to live my life how I want and what feels good to me—not according to what society expects. We shall see how it all plays out.

And, lastly, I want to share a story from the first semester of college. I was commuting to school every day, and one early evening, it was pouring rain. My car suddenly broke down in the middle of a two-lane road, and I completely backed up rush hour traffic. These were the days before cell phones so I had no idea what to do. A huge truck pulled up next to me and a very muscular older man told me to get in. I almost did because I had no idea what to do! Suddenly, a woman drove up and told me to get in her car. I jumped in. She drove me all the way home to my parents' house and dropped me off. I never got her name or saw her again. Somehow, in my mind, she was an angel saving me from some serious trouble. There has to be a good reason why that happened. I'm still trying to find that out.

(And one more story, I just can't resist. In my last year of college, I was driving on that same road and my muffler gave out. It was dragging. I drove to a side road and parked not knowing what I should do. I randomly knocked on a person's house and a young man answered the door. I explained the situation and he yanked the muffler off and tossed it over the fence to a neighbor's backyard. I said thanks and drove away with a very loud rumbling engine!)

Epilogue

Dating Stories: April 2012 – February 2014:

When I decided to move out, I signed up for Match.com right away. My self-esteem was in the toilet and I really wanted to see if a dude would want to date me: a 39-year-old, single woman with a child. Granted, I hadn't dated since 1998 and, shit, times have changed! So, here we go with all my crazy stories... (All names are anonymous, and, yes, every single word is true.)

I'll start with Meet ups #1 and #2...

The first person I met was from Match.com. He was a cute Indian dude, but proceeded to tell me how dating online was just about sex. I only met the guy for 30 minutes and the whole time he told me how many one-night stands he had and then asked if I wanted to go home with him. Very scary.

That same night, I went to go meet another guy from Match. Nice enough guy, but a drink somehow ended up in a full dinner date. The staff thought it was a special occasion, and it wasn't (complete with a bottle of wine on ice). The guy was decent enough, but really short (my height) and I wasn't attracted to him. So I just played up my impending divorce. It was a nice conversation but during the dinner I found out that he had been on Match for five years and I was his first date. I didn't know what to say to that. I felt bad, but at the same time I felt like I was duped. CLEARLY, I had no idea what I was doing.

I did meet two good Match.com dudes at the beginning.

I met a guy from the Virginia suburbs. He seemed like a great dude. In April 2012, I got into it with the Ex over text during work so after work I went to a bar near my work and proceed to drink. I was so ticked at the Ex that I was beside myself. Good god, I think I talked to every random man that night, but thankfully, the dude came out to meet me. He got my ass home and away from "the feeding sharks" around me (investment bankers). We are still in touch today, and he is the one guy that guided me through the initial divorce process. I'm grateful for knowing that guy. I really am.

I went to Orlando with my sister in May 2012. She had a conference and I figured I could relax by the pool. I texted/talked with the second good Match guy while I hung out at the pool. He absolutely understood what I was going through. He listened, understood, and taught me how to use my misery to gain random hugs at bars. We met up when I got back in town, but realized we are better as just friends. I don't see him much these days as he is dating just like I am and getting through life, but I can say in the beginning, he was one of the few I knew that got my situation. I wish him well and hope we can still be friends, even if just text buds.

I quickly learned that dudes can type and be funny on their profiles but damn, they really are different people in person. I got sushi with a Match dude ($77.77 guy) but he was so dry, not fun, and completely stiff. Possibly because he was also getting out of a marriage and unsure of dating. I was too but I don't lie in my profile. Anyway, what I remember is a random question he asked me. "What do you like to do?" and I just stared at him blankly. I had no idea and felt like an idiot not knowing! I guess after a 14-year relationship you get so used to being with the other person, and then add in constantly providing for my daughter that I really had no idea what I liked. Slowly in my journey of two years to get divorced, I've learned what I like and what I dislike. Rediscovering yourself at 39/40 years old is quite interesting to say the least!

The first guy I felt a real connection was a guy that I knew was in DC for only a few months. He was going to move to NYC. His profile said he laughed a lot, so I said, let's meet for a drink and see whose laugh was better. It was a happy hour than became a 21-hour date. Happy hour moved to dinner, dinner moved to going to see music at Madams Organ, and then I invited him over. I don't know, we just got a long really well and it was easy. He stayed over and in the morning we just talked and cuddled and it was really hard for both of us to let go. I remember him leaving around 1 p.m. and as he left, he asked if there was there something between us. I said yep, and he asked if I wanted to hang out again that night. I had to go meet the $77.77 guy for that date so I couldn't. We set to meet for brunch on Sunday just to see if the magic was still there. Yep, it was still there. I really enjoyed his company, and like I did with the Ex, I quickly felt things for him. Now I understand that it was just that I liked how I felt about myself when I was with him. It was NOT love. But I was not aware of that then, and proceeded to sort of freak out, pressuring him for more time. He was upfront about moving to NYC in the first place, and I knew that. However, I was so fresh from moving out that I was looking to grab onto something and, at the time, he was the perfect fit. In time, he moved to NYC and I'm not in touch with him anymore. I learned a lot from that dating experience about how it's much easier for men to keep sex at an even keel. Now there absolutely was a connection, and right before he moved we had dinner and ended up back at my place... the kind of situation where you open the door and clothes are ripped off. Very intense. But maybe that's it, something that intense can't be sustained for the long run. Go figure...

I forgot! I met up with a guy the first night I moved out into my apartment. That was interesting. Met him at a wine bar right near my place. Nice, cute guy, but damn, I quickly realized he had some whack thoughts on women. I only saw him a couple more times but here is his take on dating (via email):

Him:
Hate to break it to ya, but ALL guys date girls for sex. It's how we are wired evolutionarily speaking. That's it, in the beginning anyway. Then we spend the next couple months trying to decide if we can put up with them. Every guy I talk to agrees with this...so don't tell 'em I told you or I could lose my man card. ;-)

Me:
Well not to judge, but that could be the reason why you were married for only a bit. Maybe you should invest in knowing the person a bit before commitment, maybe then they wouldn't just be a roommate. Just saying. Put up with them? Really???? Clearly zero respect. I don't want to know a person like that.

Good luck out there. What you don't know is there are men out there that are more spiritual and more emotionally wise and that is what I want. Sure, I have a list of men I can use for sex, but that's really all it is. It is nice to feel wanted, and I have that in a variety of fashions.

See ya. I hope somehow you end up respecting women. Honestly, maybe you man card should be revoked. You don't tell a woman that.

Him:
Our first fight.

Sorry you took it that way, I was mostly joking. Guys do want sex, #1. Have no reason to lie. Any guy that tells you something different is just lying to himself in an attempt to impress you with his "emotional wisdom". It's how we are wired. Evolution has a big head start on spiritual power. And I am very spiritual, but that all goes away when I see a great ass (like yours) walk by. As much as we believe we are human, we are all still animals to the very core.

I love women and I have a lot of respect for women, but the fact that women have accepted their independence and have progressed beyond their counterparts has destroyed any chance of the woman-man relationship to strengthen. It's heavily deteriorated, in fact, which explains the consistent and yearly increase in number of divorces (yours and mine included). 50% of adults are married right now vs. 72% in 1960.

You may be right that I didn't know my wife completely before we married, but I do now.

We may not see it in our lifetime, but we will slowly devolve back to tribes where men will lead and women will be protected. Not like now. Chivalry is dead, sadly, and women don't need protection anymore. We (men) want to provide that protection.

As a result, men have become lost, they have no role and emasculation is on the rise.

It's funny how quickly my testosterone level returned after I moved out. Physically, I can see myself transforming and I'm not really even working out much. My sex drive is through the roof.

One of the major reasons women emasculate men, unbeknownst to them, is that women are rising to a false, masculine power where competing with men and winning at all costs often becomes a woman's sole purpose of existence. The sad fact is that it comes at a much higher cost than any woman can bare in the long run. Her true feminine essence becomes masculine, which is the biggest turnoff to any man, and inadvertently emasculates him.

Thoughts out there readers? Last I heard, he was dating a woman from Eastern Europe who understood his thinking. Good for him!

I met a golfer dude and probably saw him three times. He said he loved my energy and had never met a person that says "Woot Woot!" The best part of all of that is he shared my dork love for easy listening 1970s tunes, and at one point we ended up dancing to the tunes in my apartment. Bucket list check! But in the end, he was kind of an intense guy who never had been married, so he couldn't understand the emotions I was experiencing at that time. I remember crying in front of him because I was upset about something, but couldn't express it in a way that he could understand. He just looked at me weirdly. I knew at that point that I probably shouldn't date. I enjoyed meeting people, but I was scared as hell to get close to anyone at all. I was so afraid of being burned like I felt like I was in my marriage.

I did meet a 24-year-old guy. I know, call me a cougar, but the kid was an old soul. At that time during my online dating attempts, I would ask to talk to a guy before I met up with them because I didn't want to waste time if I couldn't talk to the guy. Anyway, we chatted once or twice and he seemed very mature. He had owned his own business since he was 15. I was supposed to meet him at a bar, but I was out at a wine bar and asked him to meet me there. Oh man, he was an old soul, but looked damn young! He had no idea how to act in a wine bar, wanted a beer, and couldn't understand why the cheese plate I ordered was so small. The entire meet up ended up being a counseling session for him. He said he could relax after he made $3 million dollars. I said "Huh? What are you going to do then? You are 24, go live your life man!" I just felt bad for him as he couldn't relate to anyone his own age. I stayed in touch with him, and one day I found myself in the original bar where we met. So I texted him that. He then announced that he had a girlfriend. I said "That's awesome, how old is she?" He said "Of course you had to ask. She's 42!" I'm happy for the guy.

The next dude I had a random connection was with a Puerto Rican 34 year old lawyer (I'll call him PR). We met for dinner on U Street in DC and had a good time.

Over a few weeks would randomly meet up and hook up. There was just something about him. We never dated seriously, but I would say for a while we were a friends-with-benefits kind of thing. We are still friends to this day, and I've actually met some new friends through him. (Can I say Dewey Beach? That's a story and a half!) There still is an attraction between us, but we are sure to say it's just a friend thing now. He loves chasing women and has been known to date two different women at once. No matter, I like calling him a friend. And that we can be open and honest. He's a Gemini too and completely gets the idea of feeling like two different people. Turns out our birthdays are two days apart. Neither of us is surprised about that. (He now has a girlfriend and she has him on lockdown so I don't hear from him anymore. Not sure if I can call him a friend anymore).

I met another guy online and shocker... he ended up not being who I thought he was. He told me he ran a lot and was constantly buying new sneakers. However, when I met him, he was not a runner. I hated the way he dressed and the buttons on his short-sleeved, button-down shirt were ready to pop open. I was a little ticked off because I felt like he lied to me. I made nice and had drinks and appetizers at the bar. He was nice enough, but I only liked him from the neck up and not the sound of his voice. At some point I went to the bathroom trying to get my girlfriend to come out. I came back and told the guy that my friend was coming and I was just going to stick around. I guess he thought that meant that he was going to hang out too. So he got another beer. I began to get frustrated. I really don't like being the person to say "Ok, I'm not feeling it, gotta go." I wanted him to leave! But he didn't, so I found a small corner of the bar and hid and texted PR. Finally, the bartenders came over and asked if I was ok. I asked if he left and they said yes. Phew! Never heard from him again. However, the story goes continues... I took a cab home. I was $5 bucks short of the fare, and the cab driver proceeded to lock me in the cab and call the cops. Two cop cars arrived, agreed with the cab driver, and proceeded to watch over me as I went to an ATM to get money out. Just crazy! Thankfully, PR showed up and we had a good time.

I did actually meet a guy at bar in Dupont Circle September 2012. I really didn't like the idea of going straight home at night after work, so I would do happy hours with myself. One night I met this young, black guy originally from Baltimore. I think he was around 27. He was a child of privilege, went to private schools, and was very well connected. He was set up with a sweet apartment deal and landed a decent job. However, it was his first job and it was interesting to see how a guy who had everything handed to him as a kid, but was a bit lost in the real world. Anyway, it was a fun meeting him, and we stayed in touch and met up a couple of times. I remember how he looked at me at the bar and said "Yeah, I could date that." Random! The best was meeting up with him in the afternoon on Adams Morgan Day. We ended up watching some football games and then he invited his friends from high school to join us. The couple was cool, but as some point I was hanging out with the girl, and I wasn't sure if she thought the dude and me were a couple or not, or had any idea how old I was. Odd for sure, but fun. We bar hopped all over Adams Morgan and I distinctly remember singing the Redskins anthem in some bar when they scored a touchdown. In the end he wanted to continue on partying, but I decided to go home. He gave me a quick kiss and that was that. We text every six months or so. Good guy. Hope it all works out for him. He was fun.

Another guy I met online was a manager at a sushi restaurant. Well, as you can guess, I met him at 6 p.m. on a Saturday for casual sushi dinner. The guy was 42, a former teacher with DC Public Schools, got annoyed with teaching, and decided to get into the sushi business. All good, but then he told me he lives in a group house, they all do pot together all the time, and Saturday nights are so much better to go out because on Friday nights everyone is so tired from the work week. He was yawning too. I asked him "Who do you date … 25 year olds?" It became very awkward and after 45 minutes we just sat there in silence. Really uncomfortable. So I said, well I'm going to get another drink before I go meet my sister. He just sat there and wouldn't leave. Meanwhile I was desperately texting my sister to come meet me earlier. Finally the rain stopped so I told him that I was going to go. Suddenly Sushi Guy perked up and asked "Do you want a ride?" I asked how, and he said on my bike. Turns out the guy had a motorcycle. I had never been on a motorcycle before so I said "Fuck it. Sure, I'll take a ride". So I put on a helmet, grabbed on, and we took off on the two-block drive to where I was meeting my sister. I got off, gave him a hug, and never saw him again. So, bucket list check: I now know what it's like to be on a motorcycle. I now know it's not something I like to do. Thanks Sushi Guy!

Ah, there was one guy that I met after texting him for a few weeks. I had him meet me at a restaurant, and, damn, again he wasn't who he represented to be. I feel bad but I excused myself to go to the bathroom and just took off. I guess they call it an "Irish exit." I can't believe I did that, but again, I didn't know how to gracefully say "Dude, you are not who you said you are!"

About mid October 2012 I was ready to give up on Match.com and OKcupid.com. I had learned the following things:

1. A guys who says he's 5'7" is really 5'2" or shorter.
2. A guy who has pictures where he never shows teeth usually has jacked up teeth.

3. A guy who only has pictures of his face very well might be lying on what kind of shape he is in.

4. I will be judged by whether I want more kids or not. (I find this odd because aren't you trying to meet a potential partner rather than just someone to birth your kids?)

5. Who knew I'd get messages from dudes that said they lived in Alexandria, VA, then come to find out they are really in Africa?

6. 60% (and probably higher) of dudes online are only looking for a quick lay. And apparently the word "fun" is code for sex. I learned this quickly, very quickly!

7. I've had to be very specific in the type of man I like. Middle-aged suburban golf types just don't do it for me, at all. I learned I like the urban look much more.

8. I really am the fantasy of every 25-year-old dude. I crack up every time!

9. So much comes down to timing, location, and a spark.

10. I seem to be most attracted to divorced men with kids and who are good dads. And good dads mean their kids come first, and if you readers have kids you know that last-minute things can happen all the time. You can't get mad at a dude for breaking plans for handling his kids. You just can't. But it sure can make dating hard!

I was forever meeting dudes that were douchebags and/or not who they said they were and/or had no ability to plan ahead and/or had family stuff come up last minute.

Finally, my luck changed. I met a decent guy online late October 2012. He was separated like me, had kids, and completely understood how weird it was to be dating again after a long marriage. We were to meet the night that Hurricane Sandy hit DC. We texted the whole day. Thankfully my daughter was with her dad. I was a nervous wreck with that weather coming through. Seeing the wind howl at the screens on my windows, watching CNN all day long, it was bad. Thankfully I didn't lose power at all! But I sure as hell was worried. Anyway, we decided to meet in Bethesda the next afternoon. I appreciated that he drove all the way from the Virginia suburbs to meet me. I didn't have a car. As you might guess, we hit it off. Just being able to be myself and speak about how weird it was to date and be a parent put me at ease. We connected emotionally over both being the ones in our respective marriages that were taken advantage of and where the spouses walked away first. Over the next three weeks we saw each other maybe seven times. The best date was going to an Obama rally in Virginia. Really, really cool. I had never done that before (bucket list check!). We tailgated, stood in line for hours, and watched the rally. I remember I became quiet... thinking, I'm going to fall for this guy. I was worried.

Now, he was separated, but separated and living in the same house with his ex and kids. And since I didn't have a car he was always coming to see me. So I really didn't see how things were in his life. The holidays came around and with the kid stuff it was hard to see each other. We had planned to spend the three days around New Year's Eve playing house together at his place because his ex and the kids were going to be in New Jersey. I remember he picked me up and we went to dinner, and something immediately felt off. However, not having a car or alternate plans I just went with it. When we got to his place, it sunk in more. Yes, they were separated in where each slept, but other than that, their lives were very much intertwined. I knew by the end of the three days I was going to have to say see ya for a few months so he could get his stuff together. New Year's Eve night we went shopping at Whole Foods, made a nice dinner, and rang in 2013. It was a very nice evening. The next day we went to a movie and his ex texted him to say she was coming home a day early. So everything in his home had to be cleaned. He was running around like a mad man. He drove me home, and we loosely made plans to see each other sometime in the next two weeks. Apparently when he got home his ex saw two champagne glasses and went off at him, basically ordering him to move out by March. I told him that maybe that is what he needed to do. He texted... maybe. And from that I knew the guy had not moved on. I really wanted to have a download of a conversation and explain how I felt about things, but he got the flu and was sick for two weeks straight and I never saw him again. That one stung really badly. He was the first guy who I let my walls down to, and who understood my situation. I felt I had been slapped in the face! I needed a New Year's Eve redo.

Now it was January 2013 and in the middle of winter, I was working crazy hours due to end of the year end crap at work and had no boyfriend. I tend to hibernate in the winter, so it kind of sucked. I would take baths every night, listen to Pandora, and just think, think, think. A couple of times I was like, damn it, I'm going to get a babysitter just to meet people. Ah, very bad idea. I think I was desperate to meet a guy and was willing to pay 100 bucks to a babysitter to go out. I learned quickly. The two times I did that, I had to stand both guys up... so sad but here are the crazy stories.

Four-Inch-Heel Guy – I had actually talked with this guy before and I liked his energy, so I figured paying for a babysitter was worth it to just get out of the house and relax somewhere. As I was leaving to meet him, I get his text "I hope you have four-inch heels on and look slutty." I wrote back that, no, I have boots and a skirt on. Of course he then asked "How high are the heels?" So I got on the Metro and I started fuming. Are you kidding me? I'm paying a babysitter to hang with a guy with crazy expectations? I just wanted to go out and chillax. I exited from the Dupont Circle Metro and went to a different bar to decide if I want to go meet the guy or not. I had told him that he needed to relax with the crazy comments for me to want to meet him. He kept texting things about role playing. Two guys at the bar noticed I looked worried. I showed them the texts and chit chatted with them. They ended up being really cool (friendly without expectations) and I started to have the kind of night I wanted to have. So, I was like, fuck it, I'm not showing up to meet the guy, he deserves to be stood up. After an hour or so, the guy next to me came up and covered my eyes playing a game, but I didn't get it. Then four-inch-heel guy showed up, looked me in the face, and said "I'm here!" I looked at him pointing to myself and said "No ho bag here!" He tried to argue with me, and then the two guys rose to my defense and argued back. It escalated and the guy across from me ended up standing up to the guy (getting out of his seat) and the yelling continued. Finally four-inch-heel guy left. Thank goodness I never met him. I never told him where I was. I guess he searched every Dupont Circle bar to find me. Scary! And the guy was 47 with kids, but even at that age some men can't behave like men. They are ruled by their cock and expect me to play by their rules. No thanks! I think I understand why the guy is single. (Bonus, I'm still in touch with the two nice dudes.)

Beat Me Guy – Maybe a couple of weeks later I did the same thing. I got a babysitter to meet a dude. He seemed like a nice, normal guy on the phone so I was a little excited to see him. Well, as I got to the Metro,

I texted him and said "Shoot, I have a five minute wait for the Metro. You are going to beat me there". Well, somehow that was code for him to text me back saying something about taking me back to his place, holding me down, and spanking me. I never got on the Metro, so I stood him up. Then he texted me back that I had a sense of humor failure. Problem is, I get that it might be a joke, however, I hadn't even met him yet. So I went to my local bar, Lia's, and hung out by myself. Why men have to behave like douchebags, I don't know. Expecting respect is a human right. He deserved to be stood up!

At some point in January I met my now friend W. Again it was from online, but at that point it was clear that I needed friends. I was very much scarred from what happened with the New Year's Eve dude that I wasn't eager to put myself out there again. Anyway, I met W and we got along really well, bonding again over being separated and raising kids. And unlike anyone I had known before, he lived somewhat close to me and was available to hang out. I mean I worked full time, but there were times when I had a five-day, kid-free stretch, and no friends to hang out with, so it worked really well. We would meet for happy hour and appetizers and both bitch and complain about the situations we were both working through. He became my support group. I still was in therapy (I ended up keeping the couples' therapist for myself), but having a confidant at that time that totally understood the stress and bullshit I was handling in my life was invaluable.

Things with the Ex got really bad in middle of February 2013. I remember going to a bad Valentine's party at a bar and finding out that I wasn't being invited to the same parties that all my old friends were invited. My girlfriends decided to do a girls' night dinner that weekend, and I offered to have it at my apartment, but instead they decided to do it at a restaurant in my neighborhood. That irked me because no friend ever asked how I was or how my new apartment was. That stung a lot. Then, on Sunday, I decided to treat myself to a brunch in Bethesda, and while I was eating the Ex and I got into it over email and text. I felt this rage build up and I just lost it. I couldn't take the stress of all of it anymore. I gave up.

I ended up at an empty bar in Bethesda at 4 p.m. crying and talking to my sister. She was worried about me, but couldn't miss the girl's dinner to come hang with me. So I called W and he came by. He proceeded to sit with me for probably eight hours of drinks and fries and let me bitch. It was an interesting night for sure, capped off with a patron telling me how great my laugh was and that I should sell it. We met a man with Downs Syndrome with his sister and brother in law. He was a very sweet man, living his life as best he could, and had family helping him. He gave me a big hug and gave me the bag of M&Ms he was keeping for himself in his pocket. (I still have that pack of M&Ms).

I told W, damn, I so wish I had a family like that. (I took my daughter there for lunch a couple of months back and the bartender remembered me… oops!)

Over the next few months, W and I hung out a fair amount. We had some great times and he got to see the person I really am. He helped me change the memory of my old wedding date by going to Preakness. He listened to me endlessly bitch. I listened to the details of his ordeal, as well. We became really close. He summed me up in these words:

"You're so much more than you seem at first. You try at life. You have mottos and beliefs. You live out loud and express yourself to the assholes of the world. You're kind and protective, like with that sweet girl at Preakness. You think about lyrics, not just about the song. You stand up for yourself, when, probably most others wouldn't - meaning when your friends abandoned you. You have a great laugh, and screw the people who don't like it. You embrace the underdog, where most people don't like the guy with Downs Syndrome at the bar in Bethesda. You push boundaries, like hopping the fence at Preakness. You find things like your birthday questions book and force yourself to think when others wouldn't. You are a good MOM when it's not always easy. You expose your daughter to the arts and to just fun things. Happy Birthday!"

We hooked up a couple of times but I knew we should just be friends. I couldn't invest all of me emotionally in a person going through the same stuff as me. I just couldn't. I enjoyed our time together, but slowly started to realize that instead of focusing on meeting with him, I needed to focus on myself and get my own shit together. While it was great to bitch and moan to him, it was keeping me in the cycle of divorce and drinking too much.

Things broke down when I finally got my first check from the Ex for part of the equity money he owed me. I remember the Ex giving me the check, depositing it, and going back to work and crying. I felt like I was putting him in the poor house, but it also hit at my self-esteem. I mean, he was willing to pay me a boatload of cash, but in the end, he couldn't even try couples counseling. He was already checked out. I mean, at that point I was done, but it made me feel bad. And I knew it. Anyway, W wanted to celebrate by going out and I didn't want to. I knew I was extremely vulnerable emotionally, and I told him that. But he begged and I gave in. Just like I knew, I drank way too much and at some point told him that he was no good for me. A bad scene, for sure. I felt guilty as hell, but I knew I was vulnerable. I should've stayed home.

We stopped talking for a few months, and at some point he got really angry at me for cutting him out of my life. That's when I saw his nasty side. He basically told me that I owed it to him to be his friend. But the way I saw it, hanging out with him wasn't letting me move forward in my life. I needed to get my shit together, and after a while, he was a distraction from the pain I had to go through. As I've learned, there is no way to get through loss of any kind except to go through it. You can't push it away, you can't go under it or over it … you have to go through it. And as hard as it was, I knew it had to happen that way. I wish W could have understood, but he wasn't at a place in his life to hear that from me. That was around the 4th of July.

At that point, I knew what I really needed was friends - girlfriends! So, one night I went out to meet a friend of mine who was also divorced. I met her for some kind of show put on by lawyers at a bar, the Black Cat. I had never been there before. Bucket List check! It was fun to hang with some girls and random guys would come up and talk to me. Granted they were drunk, but it still was an ego boost. For some reason I have a thing for musicians and I started dancing with some guy who said he was a guitarist in one of the bands. I loved that he could dance and swing me around and had rhythm. Definitely younger than me, but it was fun. At some point he asked if I wanted to see the back stage - damn straight I did! So we went downstairs and ended up in a small dressing room. As you might guess, we started kissing and hooking up, and after a while a mirror in the room came crashing down on my head! No joke. Clearly the spirits out there were there telling me - STOP! Get your shit together! I'm mean, really, what are the odds of that happening?

The next day I went to work and I didn't feel good so I went to the nurse thinking I had a concussion. I mean, the mirror hit me pretty hard on the head, so I guess it was possible. She told me I looked ok, but that I couldn't go home to sleep. I needed to stay up and have someone check on me the next morning. I completely broke down in tears because I didn't have anyone. I made a call to W and the voicemail I left him was pure panic. Anyway, he agreed to meet me in Georgetown. I hated that I had to ask him, but I had no one else and he wasn't working at the time. He was the only one who understood and got it. I walked to Georgetown from my office and by the time I got there I felt so much better. Turns out I wasn't feeling bad because of a concussion, I was having a low-grade panic attack.

W and I had a good time, but in the end it became a counseling session for him, and at some point in the middle of our time together, he broke down. I didn't understand. Then he told me that he loved me. Quite uncomfortable because I didn't feel the same way, and I knew he was just projecting feelings on me - he didn't love me. I went home at 7 p.m. and within 30 minutes, he was calling me and begging me to let him come over and to stay so he could watch over me. I couldn't do that, as it was going to send mixed messages. Again that fueled some nastiness from him. It was hard, but I knew it was better for us not to hang out. Now as I write this in February 2014, we are email buddies. I suppose we lean on each other in that way.

I haven't seen him for six months. I think he finally understands that being friends is best.

In June 2013 there was a huge event at work celebrating the scholars that were supported by the company. I loved it. It was so inspiring to shake the hands of those people. I loved telling them to keep up the good work! There was a huge party in the courtyard that lasted most of the day. I really didn't enjoy being around with any of my accounting coworkers, so I hung out with random people, people from IT, Treasury, or other parts of the company. I met scholars and senior people at the company and affiliates. It was a good time. I wound up telling some coworkers about getting divorced and my attempts at online dating. I was cracking them up. So I turned around and saw this hot guy (a certain somewhat high-profile celebrity) and I said, I want to meet that guy! So I walked up to him and shook his hand and said "Wow, I just loved your presentation! Really great celebrating smart people in the world!" All these girls were fawning over him trying to speak Spanish with him. The accounting folks took a picture, so I jumped in and I think I was right next to him. I returned to the coworker guys and I saw the hot guy was leaving. So I said, stay right here, I'm going to try and get that guy's number! So I ran up to him and asked, and he put his phone number and email address right in my phone and gave me a hug. All of accounting saw the whole thing happen. The coworker guys were impressed. Damn straight, I still got it! I love seeing him on TV and saying I know that guy!! (Granted, I was at a company party in NYC that summer and I saw him. Of course I had to say hello. I'm sure he thought I was a stalker, but he did recognize me. We texted a bit, but that was it. Still, bucket list check!)

Also on that NYC trip (booked to celebrate myself turning 40) I crossed off something else on my bucket list, one that I never knew was on it. I booked a massage at my hotel that was going to take place in a cabana outside. Apparently the masseuse guy thought I was hot and while it was the best massage in my life, right at the end he massaged my boobs! I didn't flinch because I was a pile of putty, but it was so random. Maybe it's an NYC kind of thing, but honestly, I wasn't expecting that! He gave me his card and said to contact him if I needed another one on my trip. So I contacted him and managed to get a second massage for free in my room. Bucket list check! Funny enough he wanted a review on Yelp, so I wrote one for him.

In mid-August, I met another online guy. I had talked to this guy a couple of times before I met him and he came across as a cool dude. So I met him in Bethesda and as soon as I met him, I knew this guy thought he was the shit! Oh God, cocky as hell, congratulating himself for having two relationships since his divorce, and looking down on me for not having one that lasted. The entire conversation was about him, him, him, and him. Sad really. At some point he asked "Oh wait, what did you say you did again? Oh wait, did I ask you?" I said no, you never asked. It just became uncomfortable. He then asked if I had any other questions for him and I just shook my head no. Douchebag! He paid the tab, looked at me, got in my face, and said "I don't know what all the eye rolls were about" and left. The bartender asked me what happened. I said, I'm not sure, I guess it was my eye rolls! From then on, I figured out that I wear my emotions on my face and apparently my face is very expressive. That said, I don't think that guy had met a woman like me. My guess is that he thought he was really good looking and that he expected me to be falling all over him. Nope. The guy was 45 and the two relationships he had were with 30 year olds. Shocker!

After I got laid off in late August 2013, my self-esteem took a nose dive again. Now granted, the day it happened probably was the best day for it to happen as I was actually feeling pretty hopeful. I didn't expect it all. (Although a week before I had a dream about being laid off, but quickly forgot about it.) Ironically, the same day I ran into an old neighbor who proceeded to tell me about the Ex's new girlfriend and that I needed to start looking better so I could get a man. I told her that she didn't know me, and, in fact, most guys think I'm sexy just the way I am.

I wanted to start doing things more things outside, like hiking, so I called a guy that was going to give me a ride to a hiking/meditation Meet Up. I never got to that meet up, but I knew this guy liked to hike, so I asked if we could go. He agreed and picked me up in his Mini Cooper. He was an older Iranian man who lived in the suburbs of Virginia. We took a four-hour hike and ended with a nice lunch in Bethesda. He had his sunglasses on the whole day, so I realized that I didn't really see who he was until I looked into his eyes at lunch. He was cute! Had a deep voice with an accent, and when he smiled he looked a bit like Matt Lauer. It was an interesting lunch. I really enjoyed talking to him.

After that we never went hiking again, but on random days we would take long walks, do lunch, or hang out because he had his own business from home and could move meetings/calls around. I could talk to him for hours and no drinking was involved. He understood me and I felt weirdly attracted to him. We hooked up a few times. We discussed it being a friends-with-benefits thing, but somehow he couldn't keep it at that level. A couple of times he freaked out at me for having plans, and at that point I knew I couldn't have that stress in my life. I didn't want to be involved with someone when I might disappoint them in some way. I didn't have a car and I was living my life. I was enjoying my freedom and I wasn't going to be tied down.

In the end, I've learned that sex screws things up. He was a friend to me, but he wanted more than what I could give. Granted, he saw me at really low points in my life. He's the only one who offered to come help me the night of my second move in late November 2013. I remember that night vividly. I was surrounded by boxes, all by myself, with no one to help me. I just broke down and cried. He came over and I cried on his shoulder and hugged him. It was very raw, something I really needed that night, but in the end way too intimate. I couldn't handle it. I told him I was going to NYC over Thanksgiving with my college friend of 20 years to see a taping of the Daily Show. He freaked out at me again saying that I never wanted to stay the night with him. Again, I just had to let that one lie. Sucks. I think we are still friends as we both wish each other well. But I haven't seen him since.

A random story that I have to include is from my trip to Nashville in October 2013. It was a trip I booked and paid for before I was laid off, so I had to go. I woke up one morning and decided I needed a massage to chill out. I called the nearest place and it said it had two locations, so I picked the closest one. It took me awhile to find, but when I did I was shocked. It was a one-room massage place. Apparently it was the adjunct one for overflow of the other location. So I walk in and I see this hot Jon Bon Jovi look alike sitting there. I was confused and asked him if this was the place. And he had this southern drawl and was just looking at me. I started to sweat as we started to talk and he asked if I'd like a glass of wine? (A glass of wine/relaxation beforehand was advertised on the website.) I said yes and that I was really confused about what I should I be doing. He said several times "you can do whatever you want to do." So, we were chit chatting and I came to find out that he's a singer/songwriter in some band that was making a comeback. I learned about his life on the road and when he comes home to his ranch with his dogs. Finally he suggested the massage start, so he closed the door and locked it and I went behind the curtain. It was so odd, I was there to relax but was so keyed up because 1) he was superhot, 2) I wasn't sure if the NYC massage thing would repeat itself, and 3) the guy was a stranger and I was locked in a room with him. Turns out it was a fine massage, definitely not one of the best. It almost felt like he was improvising, but it was totally professional. I paid and walked out with him. I shook his hand, said thanks, and he told me the name of his band. I can't remember it now, but it was interesting going to Nashville and actually talk with someone in the music biz. Turns out, just as they say, most people in Nashville are singers/songwriters in some form. Who knew?

Sometime that fall I ended up meeting a really cool guy (from online... again). See, by now my expectations of anyone I met online was very, very low so perhaps I was relaxed. We met up for dinner in Dupont and sparks flew, at least on my side. A lot of good, innocent flirting. After dinner I took him to Kramerbooks for a drink, and then he asked if he could drive me home. I remember him taking my hand as we were walking – very intimate. We got to his garage, into his car, and then I asked if I could kiss him. Needless to say, we started making out in his car and ended up in the back seat. I felt like I was a teenager! I'll say it... bucket list check! Against my better judgment, we went back to my place and the sex was great! His job was in Dupont, so we started to hang out on Wednesday nights.

The guy lives in the Maryland suburbs and has kids. Not the best location for dating someone. Every time I saw him I would sort of push him and tell him he needed to find a girl where he lives. I was starting to like him too much. It was hard for me to see him one day every two weeks. Every time I saw him, I felt that pull towards him. Of course right when I met him he was in the middle of accepting a new executive position which was a pretty high profile gig and he wasn't going to be working in the city any more. I didn't have a car and because he was so busy, we barely saw each other. However, when we hung out it was great, the sex was great and I scratched a couple of things off my bucket list. (Having sex in my empty new apartment and on my balcony in mid-November was HOT!) I remember in early December we finally hung out in Bethesda on a Saturday evening and I thought for sure he was kicking me to the curb, but nope, there still was that same spark. I tried to push him away, but had these weird expectations. But just like the New Year's dude, the holidays came and with his work and busy schedule I ended up not seeing him after that. Kinda stinks.

How It's Going - Early 2014

So now its 2014 and no casual sex and I'm living my life, but horny as hell. I so wish that I had a good friend with benefits! (Or a good hug. I feel like there should be some sort of service that I could call every now and then to get that hug. For now, massages are my go to.) But it feels good to be good so I'm trying, really trying. One week until my divorce is finalized and I'm in Miami for a couple of days because I can. (I've never been able to travel in the winter because of work.) I made an impression on the room service guy and got a free breakfast out of it and the pool guy gave me his number. He seemed nice enough and told me I was a triple threat - funny, down to earth and cute. Who knew?? Another guy told me "I've never met anyone like you before in my life!" Damn straight! Love, love, love unsolicited compliments.

At the end of the day, I feel the dark clouds of SHIT lifting, I feel HOPE sinking in and you know what, being 40 and single ain't so bad. I'd rather be by myself rather than stuck in a bad relationship. Feels damn good realizing that! I get compliments on my laugh wherever I go. I was recently carded by a waitress who really thought I was under 30. Somehow random people remember who I am (including a cab driver I hadn't seen in six months, but after a five-minute cab ride to take my daughter to school, he was telling everyone he knows how great a mom I was and how he wants to parent like me).

I've been called a great first date and in January 2014 I went to Madams Organ where as soon as my friend and I showed up, two 30 year olds wanted to dance with me (even though there were two slutty dressed girls there kissing each other). I now am the one to help newly separated men or women navigate the crazy land of divorce. I'm happy to be in that position.

I've manage to survive four major lifetime events in the span of two years (moving, divorce, being laid off from my job, and moving again). This is the first time in my life where I am truly on my own with no one by my side helping me and I'm ok! I don't need someone to make me feel ok. I will be the one to take care of me.

I can travel by myself now with no problems (I've been to Miami, Puerto Rico, NYC, Charleston South Carolina, Nashville, and Key West. I'm going to Jazz Fest 2014, and maybe I'll take an international trip in the summer.) I am also comfortable traveling with my daughter. But no lie, being surrounded by nuclear families is still hard for me. However, when I took my daughter to Disney World during the summer of 2013 one of the days she told me that it was the best day of her life. I just cried. It was hard, but I feel proud I can give her those experiences. Now she didn't understand that it was happy tears but needless to say, I was thrilled.

I really have no idea where the hell I will end up or work, but as I've told others, I think I'm finally comfortable being uncomfortable, in every type of situation. I finally trust myself and the decisions I make, even if in the end it might be a mistake or perceived as wrong by someone. I'm not your average girl. I'm not your average mom. And at a New Year's Eve 2014 dinner with relative strangers I was asked "What are you good at?" I automatically said "I'm good at being ME!!!" WOOT WOOT!

This little light of mine, I'm gonna let it shine! Shine baby shine!

I lied – Last story, just a quick one:

I met my first boyfriend was when I was 16. He was 19 and yeah, we met at Domino's. YIKES!

After a year we broke up and I lost track of him. I knew he went into the Army, but I was never clear if he was still alive or anything. I was finally made contact with him over Facebook during the turmoil. I told him that I was getting divorced, that it sucked, and he says:

"You will get through it and if you're still like the way you were when I knew you, you're strong enough to come out on top. You've always been strong even if you didn't feel it or see it I always saw it."

Wow… hearing this from someone who knew me when I so young and innocent just confirms that I should and will believe in myself from now on!

The End

(Okay – I thought that was the end of my book/story, however, the last few days have proven that the story has a bit more to be told!)

I was scheduled to get officially divorced on February 13, however, as luck would have it, a snow storm shutdown DC and everything, including the court, was closed. So I was told by the court clerk that if this happens, the cases are pushed to the next day. The storm was really bad on the 13th, but all I could think of was, are you kidding me, I'm going to get divorced on Valentine's Day? (Turns out, February 13 was the same day in 2012 when I broke my left hand, the Ex let me fend for myself and worked late, and came home to say "Oh, it is broken!" I got my cast on February 14. I chose the color green. The doctor had suggested red – NOPE!)

The Ex tracked through the snow to get me the divorce docs on the 13th. I managed to climb over four piles of snow to get to my local bar to talk with my girlfriend that night. Thank goodness I stayed out late instead of feeling nervous at home. I woke up to find out that court opened at 10 a.m., and our hearing was scheduled at 9:30 a.m. So I really wasn't sure if it was rescheduled. The Ex couldn't go to court that day so I was going to go to court by myself. I was getting my daughter at 11 a.m., so I knew the timing was too tight. I called to reschedule and found out that the Ex really had to be there because he was the plaintiff. So, it turns out that my fright on February 13 was a completely waste of time. I tried to reschedule, but the court had to contact the Ex and he was completely unavailable all of February 14, and by the time he called later that day, court was adjourned. So as I write this, it's Sunday, February 16, and I won't know until Tuesday February 18, when it will be rescheduled. Frustrating as hell. I really need this to happen to move on with my life.

I went on a random date on February 12, probably because I wanted something to do and I didn't want to be home thinking about how the court date was going to go down. He was a complete douchebag! He smelled like cigarettes, looked at his phone whenever I talked, started yelling at me like I was his ex, told me it was my fault for being in the situation I was in (saying I should've hired a big-time lawyer and sucked the Ex dry of cash), and criticized me for sending my daughter to DC Public Schools. I think I looked flabbergasted the whole time. When he finally left the owner of the place looked at me and said "Worst Date Ever." No kidding! I know I just met him for a distraction but damn, that's what I get to deal with? Kind of nuts! Of course I had to write about it.

The deed is done - (Bucket list check!)

The deed was done at 9:30 a.m. on Wednesday February 19, 2014. Unfortunately, I didn't find out the date until the day before, so my idea of having a divorce party was completely nixed. Grrr! But my sister came with me, I got a high five from the security guard, the court told me to be quieter since my laugh was so loud, and by 10:15 a.m. it was over. I had a nice lunch with my sister, got an awesome massage at Nusta Spa and met a random man in the relaxation room, then went to Kramerbooks to do my final writing for this book, but got sidetracked talking to an older man looking for a dance partner who told me that laughing out loud was unbecoming. Random. I went home to no hug or date waiting for me, and that part was sad (and yeah, I cried a bit), but probably necessary at this point in my life. It's important I understand that I am on my own, and that I can handle it. Cheers! Here's to me living life on my own terms!

It's done! Thank goodness! Moving on and upward ...

Thanks for reading my Road to Me 2.0 story!

Epilogue 2:

Song Lyrics

These are songs that have moved me in one way or another over the past two years. Just short pieces of the lyrics (if I wrote them all down it would add 30 pages to the book), but at the end of the day they speak to me, and as much as I feel my life can be told in song, I decided that this book had to be written as such. But it is very much complemented by these songs. I really do love all of these songs. Props to all who wrote, produced, and sang these songs. God damn I love music! Enjoy!

Turning Tables - Adele - I played this at HIGH VOLUME many times between March and June 2012 before moving out.

Close enough to start a war,
All that I have is on the floor,
God only knows what we're fighting for,
All that I say, you always say more,

I can't keep up with your turning tables,
Under your thumb, I can't breathe,

So I won't let you close enough to hurt me
No, I won't ask you, you to just desert me
I can't give you what you think you gave me

It's time to say goodbye to turning tables

Under haunted skies I see, ooh,
Where love is lost, your ghost is found,
I braved a hundred storms to leave you,
As hard as you try, no, I will never be knocked down

Thinking 'Bout Somethin – Hanson: Again, I played this at HIGH VOLUME many times between March and June 2012 before moving out.

Well I gave you love, you know it
So when did you outgrow it
And decide that you would find another man?

Well you've been out there shakin
The tail the boys are chasing
When you get home you think I'll be the bigger man

I've been thinkin bout somethin
I've been thinkin bout somethin other than you

Well I've run out of patience
For this sticky situation
You won't find me crying that we're through

You didn't have to do what you did
But I thank you it ended like this
Cause the love I've got it better than what you gave

Missy Higgins - Where I Stood: I spent a night staying up until 6 a.m. in August 2012 listening to songs like this.

I don't know what I've done
Or if I like what I've begun
But something told me to run
And honey you know me it's all or none

There were sounds in my head
A little voice is whispering
That I should go and this should end
Oh and I found myself listening

'Cause I don't know who I am, who I am without you
All I know is that I should
And I don't know if I could stand another hand upon you
All I know is that I should

'Cause she will love you more then I could
She who dares to stand where I stood

A Sorta Fairytale - Tori Amos

on my way up north
up on the ventura
i pulled back the hood
and i was talking to you
and i knew then it would be

a life long thing
but i didn't know that we
we could break a silver lining

and i'm so sad
like a good book
i can't put this day back
a sorta fairytale
with you
a sorta fairytale
with you

and i rode along side
till you lost me there in the open road

When a Heart Breaks – Ben Rector: Funny, I saw his show at the 9:30 Club and very randomly ended up meeting him and his band on the street after the show. I was able to tell them that I woke up to his CD every morning. Bucket list check!

I woke up this morning
And I heard the news
I know the pain of a heartbreak
I don't have answers
And neither do you
I know the pain of a heartbreak

This isn't easy
This isn't clear

And you don't need Jesus
Til you're here
Then confusion and the doubts you had
Up and walk away
They walk away
When a heart breaks

I heard the doctor
But what did he say
I knew I was fine about this time yesterday
I don't need answers
I just need some peace
I just need someone who could help me get some
sleep

Kissing a Fool – George Michael: This came up a lot
when things ended with New Year's Eve dude. I felt
so stupid. It's the song that makes me think of sitting
around a piano in NYC in winter—romantic and full
of meaning. Love it!

You are far,
When I could have been your star,
You listened to people,
Who scared you to death, and from my heart.
Strange you that you were strong enough,
To even make a start.....
But you'll never find, peace of mind,
Til you listen to your heart.

You are far.
I'm never gonna be your star.
I'll pick up the pieces, and mend my heart.
Maybe I'll be strong enough,
I don't know where to start.
But I'll never find, peace of mind,
While I listen to my heart.

Strange that I was wrong enough,
To think you'd love me too...........
You must have been.........
Kissing................................... a fool

Freedom '90– George Michael: Theme song 2013

Think i'm gonna get me some happy
I think there's something you should know
I think it's time i told you so
There's something deep inside of me
There's someone else i've got to be
Take back your picture in a frame
Take back your singing in the rain
I just hope you understand
Sometimes the clothes do not make the man

All we have to do now
Is take these ties and make them true somehow
All we have to see
Is that i don't belong to you
And you don't belong to me

Freedom
You've gotta give for what you rake
Freedom
You've gotta give for what you take
Heaven knows we sure had some fun boy

Out Tonight – Musical Rent : Oh yeah, I was 39 and I was going to relive some of my 20's damn it!

What's The Time?
Well It's Gotta Be Close To Midnight
My Body's Talking Me
It Says, 'Time For Danger'
It Says 'I Wanna Commit A Crime
Wanna Be The Cause Of A Fight
Wanna Put On a Tight Skirt And Flirt
With A Stranger'

Let's Go Out Tonight
I Have To Go Out Tonight
You Wanna Play?
Let's Run Away
We Won't Be Back
Before It's Christmas day
Take Me Out Tonight

Lovely – Sara Haze: Great, great, great lyrics!

I don't wanna be her
I just want to be little old me
Shouldn't have to think
Who am I suppose to be today
And what give you the right
To tell me who I should be
Who gave you that right

Cause I, I feel lovely
Just the way that I am
Yes I feel lovely
The way that I am

I need that to be enough for you
Need that to be enough for you
Cause it's enough for me
It's enough for me

I'm I suppose to give up everything I am
Just to make you happy
I thought I was the one you
Always wanted me to be
It turns out I'm just little old me
I'm just little old me
And that's fine by me

Something To Believe In – Parachute: I wake up like this. Kind of spoke to me.

You wake up every morning looking for your answer
You're waiting for your sign
While Jeremiah's on his way to tell the people
But you watch him pass you by

You walk the streets at night still looking for your reason
But you don't wanna try
You swear the world has got you backed into a corner
But no one holds your hand to walk into a fight

You swear the light is gonna find you
But it can't find you when you're waiting all the time

You say, "keep my head from going down"
Just for a little, just for a little
Watch my feet float off the ground
Just for a little, just for a little
Love, if you can hear this sound
Oh, just give me something, something to believe in

Follow Through - Gavin Degraw

Oh, this is the start of something good
Don't you agree?
I, haven't felt like this in so many moons

You know what I mean
And we can build through this destruction
As we are standing on our feet

So, since you wanna be with me
You'll have to follow through
With every word you say
And I, all I really want is you
You to stick around
I'll see you every day
But you have to follow through
You have to follow through

The words you say to me are unlike anything
That's ever been said

Oh, this is the start of something good
Don't you agree?

Kiss Me Slowly – Parachute: Very sweet song. So
what I want.

Stay with me, baby stay with me,
Tonight don't leave me alone.
Walk with me, come and walk with me,
To the edge of all we've ever known.

I can see you there with the city lights,
Fourteenth floor, pale blue eyes.
I can breathe you in.

Two shadows standing by the bedroom door,
No, I could not want you more than I did right then,
As our heads leaned in.

Well, I'm not sure what this is gonna be,
But with my eyes closed all I see
Is the skyline, through the window,
The moon above you and the streets below.
Hold my breath as you're moving in,
Taste your lips and feel your skin.
When the time comes, baby don't run, just kiss me
slowly.

Don't run away...
And it's hard to love again,
When the only way it's been,
When the only love you knew,
Just walked away...
If it's something that you want,
Darling you don't have to run,
You don't have to go ...

When You Say Nothing At All - Alison Kraaus: This is
for the one that listened to me way in the beginning
and had such a quiet way and taught me about what
it's really like to feel cared for. You know who you are.

It's amazing how you can speak right to my heart
Without saying a word you can light up the dark
Try as I may I could never explain

What I hear when you don't say a thing

The smile on your face
lets me know that you need me
There's a truth in your eyes sayin'
you'll never leave me
The touch of your hand says
you'll catch me if ever I fall
You say it best when you say nothing at all

Chances – Five for Fighting

Chances are when said and done
Who'll be the lucky ones who make it all the way?
Though you say I could be your answer
Nothing lasts forever no matter how it feels today

Chances are we'll find a new equation
Chances roll away from me
Chances are all they hope to be

Don't get me wrong I'd never say never
'Cause though love can change the weather
No act of God can pull me away from you

I'm just a realistic man, a bottle filled with shells and
sand
Afraid to love beyond what I can lose when it comes
to you
And though I see us through, yeah

Chances are we'll find two destinations
Chances roll away from me
Still chances are more than expectations
The possibilities over me

Chances, chances
Chances lost are hope's torn up pages
Maybe this time

Chances are we'll be the combination
Chances come and carry me
Chances are waiting to be taken, and I can see

100 Years – Blues Traveler

The sun is warm as the day is long
I just got the feeling I can do no wrong
I've got a long way to walk
Can't afford my next meal
I tell a few lies but my hunger is real

And It won't mean a thing in a hundred years
No, it won't mean a thing in a hundred years

Mademoiselle tell me do you play
Well, if she shakes her head, well then that's okay
I watch her walk away in haste
There's just no accounting for some people's taste

Brave – Sara Barellis: This is the song that helped me realize that moving out and onward was a brave thing to do. Props to me! (Saw her at the 9:30 Club in an acoustic performance … now that was Brave!)

You can be amazing
You can turn a phrase into a weapon or a drug
You can be the outcast
Or be the backlash of somebody's lack of love
Or you can start speaking up
Nothing's gonna hurt you the way that words do
And they settle 'neath your skin
Kept on the inside and no sunlight
Sometimes a shadow wins
But I wonder what would happen if you

Say what you wanna say
And let the words fall out
Honestly I wanna see you be brave

Everybody's been there, everybody's been stared down
By the enemy
Fallen for the fear and done some disappearing
Bow down to the mighty
Don't run, stop holding your tongue
Maybe there's a way out of the cage where you live
Maybe one of these days you can let the light in
Show me how big your brave is

The Show - by Lenka : This was when I started to let go of some anger and realize that things happen for a reason, even bad things.

I am just a little girl
Lost in the moment
I'm so scared
But don't show it
I can't figure it out
It's bringing me down
I know
I've got to let it go
And just enjoy the show

Slow it down
Make it stop
Or else my heart is going to pop
'Cuz it's too much
Yeah, it's a lot
To be something I'm not

Bruises - Train featuring Ashley Monroe: This was when I realized that most everyone has gone through rough patches, just not everyone speaks about it as openly as I do.

Haven't seen you since high school
Good to see you're still beautiful
Gravity hasn't started to pull
Quite yet I bet you're rich as hell

One that's five and one that's three
Been two years since he left me
Good to know that you got free
That town I know was keeping you down on your
knees

These bruises make for better conversation
Loses the vibe that separates
It's good to let you in again
You're not alone in how you've been
Everybody loses, we all got bruises

The next 3 songs I just love! In 3 eloquent songs they
explain my 2 years of turmoil so completely. Love it!

Frozen Over – Diane Birch

I don't know what
Happened to my heart
'coz I can't feel the beat
No, I can't feel the beat
I'm frozen over

We had it all
The thrill of the night
We danced in the madness
Lived for the fight

Lost in a truth that I can't deny
Cold as a stone, no

I can't even cry
Love is a flower
With wings of time
Ready to bloom
Ready to die

Hold On A Little Longer – Diane Birch

There's a ghost in the mirror
That looks a lot like someone
You used to know

There's a hole in your heart
That keeps getting bigger
And a fire that keeps going out
There's a light in your eyes
That keeps getting dimmer
And no one seems to hear when you shout
Hold on a little longer

Emptiness
Just fills you up
And this life
Gets too much
Take my hand
Don't let it go
You're in the darkness
But no not alone

Lighthouse – Diane Birch

Some days I'm low
And I know I'm far from home
I see my name and a rose
On a white stone
Live a little woman
Your eyes ain't meant to close
I've been walking the
Wasteland of my heart
You came and delivered me

You are a lighthouse
A lighthouse in the dark
You are a lighthouse
Callin' out, callin' out
And you hear me
SOS, SOS and you beam me
'Cos you are a lighthouse
A lighthouse in the dark

Sometimes you fall
To your knees under attack
People they run
When they see the blood
On your back

I Really Want It – A Great Big World: Theme song
2014! Such a HAPPY SONG! (In spring 2014, I saw this
band at a luncheon. So intimate and right before
they were going on a world tour. Bucket list check!)

So tell me what are we living for?
I say we chuck inhibitions
And sell our souls to rock and roll
I need to know what I'm missing

So turn it up on the stereo
Somebody light the ignition
What the hell are you waiting for?
It's time to make a decision

I'm feeling the world go round
It's spinning me upside down
I'm finally homeward bound
I'm not giving up
It's crawling under my skin
And I don't care if I sin

I really want it,
I really want it,
I really want it right now
I really want it right now

Thanks:

Cheers to my new friends that I've made since I moved out. You were tremendous support in making me feel like I wasn't alone, wasn't the only one going through hard times, and generally let me bitch and complain. You know who you are. I hope with this book I am paying it forward in a little way...

Love and Hugs – Me 2.0.

About the Author:

Me 2.0 lives in Washington DC with her daughter 50 percent of the time. She spends her time making lemonade out of lemons and is currently contemplating a career in coloring outside of the lines. And biggest thing of all, she's enjoying the show called Life. ☺

It's taken her 40 years but now she knows how she should be treated (per the wise words of a dear friend):

The significant relationships in her life will not always be perfect, but they should always be honest, respectful and free of bullying, mind games, and anxiety. She should always know where she stands.

True that!